What I Would Not Part With

Poems of First Times

Bruce Jennings

Copyright ©2023 Bruce Jennings

All Rights Reserved

I could give all to Time except—except
What I myself have held. But why declare
The things forbidden that while the Customs slept
I have crossed to Safety with? For I am there,
And what I would not part with I have kept.
—Robert Frost, "I Could Give All to Time"

Death belongs to life as birth does
The walk is in the raising of the
Foot as in the laying of it down.
—Rabindranath Tagore, *Stray Birds*

To Margaret A. Jennings (1950-2020)
No longer with me in some ways, with me even more so, in others.

Margaret Ann Machulis Jennings was born and grew up in Oklahoma. We met in 1970, were married in 1972, and celebrated our forty-eighth wedding anniversary a few weeks before her death. "Celebrating" is a word that springs back when pressed down. More subdued than earlier ones, to be sure, that last anniversary was nonetheless a felt celebration of a lifetime together. A lifetime does not disappear just as soon as you know for certain that the end of it for one of you is near. It does not even disappear when that end comes, for you have kept what you would not part with. That she lived and what she did made the world better for many people. I hint at that catalogue in the final lines of my opening poem, "Deep Sleep." For me, the world shared with her was my everything. Still, these poems are not only about loss, although awareness of absence and grief are my constant companions as I walk among trees. More importantly, these poems call attention to how things we must do for the first time permeate our lives. And how often we are surprised by the joy that comes from doing them.

Contents

Deep Sleep 1
A Morning of Fleeing Nows 3
Beautiful Swimmers 7
The Time of Our Lives 9
There and Gone 11
Beneath the Bone 12
The Punctuation of Our Eyes 13
Inland Sea 14
The Art of Lingering 16
Lost Child 18
The Children of War 20
Indiana Funeral 22
When Burning Wood Crackles in a Certain Way 24
Closely Watched Husbands 28
Achieving Cancer Mastery 30
Uphill Speech 32
After You 34
Past Participle 35
At My Door 37
To-Do List 39
A Country for Old Men 41
The Irony of Loneliness 46
Removing In 47
Nightname 48
Suddenly is Considerate 50
Nashville Snow 51
Living Will 53
Claim the Space 56
Holding on to Morning 57
The Way of All Bruising 59

Random Walk	62
Remontancy	64
Widower's Watch	65
Acknowledgments	67
About The Author	69

Deep Sleep

Your sleep was deep, breath shallow.
Above you, I stood watching
yearning to lie on
the bed beside you.
Too high a railing
too many tubes wires
tangled between us now.

It was fifty years ago I first
got into bed with you.
After that, we'd always banter,
—*Is that you?* you'd say
—*Who else might it be?*
—*How long do we have?* you'd ask
—*Not long.*

You were not drowsy then
or dying. Fifty years.
I did the math
I had nothing else to do.

One day you roused
took a cube of Jello
reached for the
sipper straw waving in a glass

I guided it to your mouth.

Fifty years and now, amid
so many machines
the sipper straw seemed to me
one of mankind's best inventions.

After you had gone back to sleep,
I watched as all your
achievements from before
filed past and went out of the room,
leaving you with nothing
but the gown on your back,
and the straw in your glass,
and what I would remember.

Next morning as my warm hand
caressed a cheek gone cold,
I saw grief loitering in branches by the window.
Grief told me that
what I would not part with, I should keep.
It said the perseverance of my life
affirms the significance of yours:

You a young programmer of global climate models,
who later helped redesign the US air traffic control system,
whose love reared your son and husband and left them whole.

A Morning of Fleeing Nows

Goodbyes that day
went only one way
and I did not know
which way to turn

I made arrangements
but not choices
I had forgotten how

Longer than she stayed
I sat by her bed
hoping to hear
her breath sounds again

grief told me
to hold on,
hold on to the stillness,
for it would not last.

I sought to be still
I sought its cover
grief was not wrong,
and the stillness was swept away

by the arrival of a chaplain,
my family, and by the return
of nurses in soothing greens
walking on quiet-soled shoes.

I am not complaining.
Quiet souled women
gathered around her bed
as they had done hours

before in the moonlight
and again in the dawn,
but the arrangements now
were theirs, not hers.

Watching their oblations
I had a dream
of smoke in a mist that filled
the space of me
and time was
reduced to a mourning
of fleeing nows.

I awoke and knew
that the time of doing
was at hand. I was almost
relieved, but for the fact that
I did not know what to do.

The first act was condoling.
Taking and passing along
words exchanged like tissues
when you have no tears.

Mingling, grief had shifted away from me
and was across the room
giving my son advice,
while my young grandson
wondered what the rules
of this school might be.
The boy's mother stayed close,
glazing a figurine of memory.

The second act was departing.
The nurse stepped everyone out of the room
before the men from the funeral home
went in with their gurney

They took from me the dress
she wanted, and I had brought
I knew they would not
let me put it on her myself

They rolled her into the hallway
and turned left toward the back
while my family
turned right toward the front.

Without knowing how, I chose—
I looked left and turned right
turning my back on her.

I sit in judgment on that now
and ask if I should have gone
with her to the crematorium
where she would be so alone

I say to myself that it is better
to accompany those loved toward the future
than to follow one loved toward the past.
Myself tells me that he is not so sure.

Beautiful Swimmers

She and I swam a long way
in our crossing of the big lake.
Middle of the journey—shore behind
barely discernable, a thin line in the haze;
shore ahead, little more.

We were beautiful swimmers.
Of the solitary things we did together
it was perhaps the best.

The travel was light
smooth muscles worked
slow no motion wasted:
spirit coming in and going out,
we carried only wonder and fear;
and wore little cloth covers,
useless for the swimming,
needed only for the propriety
of returning to land.

If we do.
The weather was coming
many boats were around,
one would get us.

The time was for waiting
I floated on my back
watching the black clouds form
she clung hard to a buoy
and stared down its slimy chain into dark water.

The Time of Our Lives

Our time was not sand
but the space
to be filled
in the depressions left
as we walked barefoot on the shore.

Time was not seized
but displaced
by pressure
in the grasp
of an empty hand.

How many miles
of beach
did we walk
making tracings
erased by the sea?

How many figures
and futures
did we abandon
on that canvas
and save for later?

How many couplings
were imagined
side by side
then rolled smooth
in the time we had?

There and Gone

Freud's baby grandson Ernst delighted in
throwing out and reeling in, *Fort* and *Da*,
seeking mastery over gone and there.

I too let people off the hook,
throw them back then try to reel them in
as if connection persists.

Your shining ambivalences returning disappearances
confound my reeling quest for control.

So I stalk and marvel in hiding at your mastery—
arriving always as partially as you depart,
cloaked by cloud or shadow most of the time.

You make me howl bloodhounds bay hay riders kiss
as oceans rise.

You can turn red but are rarely blue.
Now your lunacy has brought night to noon
pressing the bright side of my sun against the dark side of your
moon.

Beneath the Bone

Her hair was entwined and his entangled.
That is the fundamental difference between them.
Not, say, the fact that she produces ova and he spermatozoa,
Nor that for him she is what makes spring days possible.
Nor that when they walk together arm-in-arm
She poses a question by pressing his bicep
And he flexes it in reassuring answer.
In seeking the single source of difference
One turns to the abundance of what is not different.
Saying if only we could sort this out.
Her hair has been lovingly braided all her life.
Her mother did this for her when she was a girl.
Now he gently brushes and braids her,
but for himself disdains a comb.
She tousles his thicket and takes delight
In running her fingers through its storm.
And stroking his scalp, after all these years,
She senses but never quite determines
What lies beneath the bone.

The Punctuation of Our Eyes

Where I once loved on faith,
snowbound now I sit
at a window reading frost,
warm within but cold without you.
Your relinquished desire
beckons me touch the skin

of pregnant clouds
breaking their water on the world
and contemplate the life of a shape
still rough-hewn in his glistening afterbirth,
amid the traces we left on each other.

Do we then but drift
amid the sights we see and die?
All the rest is in-between
the pauses and the scars,
in the punctuation of our eyes.

Inland Sea

Realization strikes and stuns.
Its natural icon is lightning,
parting the darkness behind
from the darkness ahead.

So it was, when I realized
that our life together
has been built on
animating dreads, after all.

Yours has been abandonment;
mine, rejection.
Many ways out and no way in,
a symmetry endured for so long,
constructed out of two kinds of separation.

Between us was the expanse
of an inland sea
where waves do not roll smooth
as they do across large oceans
but are serrated and jab ragged when
revealed in unwarned flashes.
So confined, how we flayed each other
in the loneliness of those waters.

Dread transfuses hatred.
I did not realize how profound
yours was for me
until your final illness had revealed
itself as final, after all.

One morning you threw words in my face
after a night of vomiting (yours)
and anxiety (mine) in place of sleep:
Why did you let this happen to me

I have a terrible tendency
to hear grammatically
and I am always wrong.
I responded as though it were a question
but it was an accusation
I had only begun to comprehend
and for which I had no answer.

The Art of Lingering

For a long time we went to bed early,
achieved an equipoise,
and sparred on equal footing.
My jabs more cerebral
your body shots more
lasting in their effects.
Yet over the long term,
we were both sparred.

We needed the dawn
of giving as good as we got.
Resisting in each other's arms
the chauvinism of ballroom dancing—
me leading and you following,
you stepping back, me toward.

We went to bed early
but did not linger long.
Afterwards, I stayed up late
reading or listening to sad songs
about the death of kings.

A great sacrifice, you felt and said,
one of many, repeated often.
Irreconcilable differences of
circadian rhythms, your Honor.

Loans never repaid, collecting interest
resentment compounded quarterly at first,
then daily. A nicely dressed collector
with no neck, paid visits, broke fingers.

Fictions of fairness
a reciprocal ruse.
I don't know how it lasted.
but I think I do
know why.

Lost Child

You never forget where you were when you heard
or could forget what you felt when you told her mother.

Taken apart, then put back;
you didn't notice your alteration
until you could not find
the moon.

You were a wasp in a spider's web
stinging furiously at death,
assaulted by memories without mercy
as you lay in the dark.

You remember the first day you dropped her off at school,
how it feels as she clings and pleads with you to stay.
You listen to her lament as the teacher leads her away,
and speak to yourself with jagged self-reproach.

You linger, options open, rather than leave,
you spy unobserved at her classroom window,
you find her bathed in attention, swimming in life.

Then you know the transit of sorrow
and how to find your way to solace.
But as for grief, it never sleeps,

but lingers with you at the school window
and visits you and your wife on that day each year
when grief sits on the back of your hand
as you brush aside a tear on her mother's cheek.

The Children of War

The children of war stare out of wastebaskets
throughout the land with jagged eyes.
They speak from the forgotten.

Peering from these envelopes are eyes
with a gaze so steady and relentless that
they see with curled edges.

The boy with red hair baptized at a font of blood
flowing from his older brother's chest,
pooling in the gutter.

The naked girl running on the dry road,
her small feet setting off little explosions of dust,
fleeing from men who would clothe her in fire.

The baby-of-bones, distracted for a moment,
turns away from a mother's withered breast
to face the allure of a wave, a whistle, a bright thing.

I cannot meet their gaze for long.
I hide from these children in the eyes of my own child.

They find me nonetheless.
They arrive in gravid bellies
stamped with my address,
and with a sharp edge, I deliver them.

Does severing entail connection?
If he who puts them in is gone,
is he who takes them out, the father?

I kiss the photographs.
Where all is flat and bottomless
I ache to shape.

What if I cannot make these children solid?
Then I shall make them into a poem with curled edges.

The children of war have no hand to hold but God's.
They say to listen closely is to hear from far away.
They say metonymy matters more than metaphor.
They say, for each embrace, a pair of empty arms.

Indiana Funeral

Death in the family returned me
to a land chiseled flat by glaciers
beneath an ice-age sky
as they gouged the Great Lakes out.

I wore the old Protestant amour.
I was beyond the usual motives that lead one
to attend a funeral—curiosity, loneliness, nostalgia—
so I said, but in truth these feelings are always with me
like insistent cats that smell a fish.

Truly missing from the marrow of my life
is the courage to give myself to others
in a situation without remainder.

Ending long separation opened a window
through which I glimpsed people of trust
who saw past the falsely magnified
and could find what I had forgotten
in the reflection of wide, deep lakes.

Respects paid, I returned to New York,
jagged land of Momus, city of my opaque life,
again shutting windows and finding fault,
I felt myself shopworn from being turned inside-out

by those searching for a weak seam,

a shoddy stitch, or uneven hem,

hiding somewhere to take advantage.

When Burning Wood Crackles in a Certain Way

You can't go home again.
How would you know if you did?

We spend our lives in halls of mirrors
wandering from one reflection to another
searching for our true one, which,
if found, will take you home.

Questions flush like quail
as I walk through the field toward the house.

Must the wandering be aimless
and happiness haphazard?
Can the search be organized?
Does finding the way home
require already being there?

Can we take such questions home
with us or does being home mean
already having answered them?

That we talk at all is not simple.
What we talk about is not simple.
Home is not a simple place.

It is often easier to be in transit
away from or back to it
than to be there.

Coming home is less arrival
than achievement,
less cessation than surcease,
home is rest walking.

Coming home is attaining a stride
with ease of movement
as when you find the hidden current
of the water or the land
and surrender to its undertow
accepting its flow and its penance.
Every homecoming ends one penance
and begins another.

The latch turns
the door opens
the threshold is crossed
as the location of half-forgotten rooms
makes sense again.

Deeds done come back
down hallways and stair steps,
they join you on couches and floors

as you gaze into winter log fires
before which you knew your
first vivid joy, later true heartbreak,
each recalled whenever needful
and sometimes when not welcome.

When burning wood crackles
in a certain way, or perhaps it is
the returning scent
that took you unaware then
and cannot be brushed back
into the ashes of the grate now.
Guided by whispered echoes,
led or scent to bed, you cross to safety.

To move around a home
capable of being dwelt in
is to find hurtful things
you thought lost
right where you left them.
Like tin soldiers, they remain,
they have not forsaken the watch
for they are not merely patient,
they are patience.

Having reached the back of the house
you find that needful things abide—
potable water
edible food
a cornered place of sleep
the warmth of morning sun on bare skin
the relief of having something to say
and someone to say it with.

Here desire, longing, remorse
find respite from both fight and flight,
in rest from spite, in a journey accomplished
and a homecoming begun.

Closely Watched Husbands

They came the day after her brain surgery.
They looked into his wife's ICU room.
A close couple, good friends for many years.
Perhaps that's why they came.
Why would anyone come?

The woman had the same kind of tumor his wife did,
albeit growing on her spine instead of on her brain.
She was receiving radiation treatments on a lower floor
of the same massive hospital, which stood solid
on granite cliffs above the Hudson River.
Stood solid, housing human beings who could not.

Two older women with little to choose between them,
separated by the floor-to-ceiling glass wall of his wife's room.
That was a place of refuge between the frailty of her flesh
and modern surgery's response, which had opened
a portal in her skull, sealed over now with a titanium plate.
The ICU suspends you between being alive and not.
But she didn't lose her hair then
and now she doesn't set off metal detectors,
and she says. "Well, that's not nothing."
Not nothing is what she has.

In a world that was cold but not cruel, he had been struggling
with its concerto of deprivation and its danse macabre.
Muscle control on the right side, gone;
on the left, intact for now.
Syntax shattered by aphasia, prognosis uncertain.
Cognitive and affective sequelae, to be determined.

He stood now with the woman and her husband
in a hallway patrolled by nurses, and by the muted sounds
of machinery pumping and the elemental whooshing of the air.
These hums were interrupted periodically by harsh alarms,
buzzers crying out in anxious tones, like angry mother birds
scolding the sharp-sighted owl who slowly
circles and searches overhead.

The woman died first, a few years before his wife did,
and at the time he watched her husband closely to learn
how to behave when left alone in the waiting room,
as the shared life you have taken for granted
disappears through a closing door and into the river
of ancient indifference visible below the hospital window
with its priceless view.

Achieving Cancer Mastery

His wife lay reduced. An object of intensive surveillance.
The work of the tumor and the work of her surgeon
left her silent for a time, and he lost his own articulation.
She borrowed time, but tumors are loan sharks
who charge compound interest due at an uncertain date.
Another price was demanded by the surgeon.
This one could be paid if her brain
had the resilience to bounce back
and if their love for each other could raise the cash.

The part of his brain that is the mind pondered this.
It weighed recovery and diminishment, one in each palm,
and he wondered how blind justice would apportion them.
The part of his brain that is the heart was terrified by those
proceedings and could not bear to look them in the face
or grasp them with its bare hands.

As he walked back toward the elevators to return home,
he thought how his wife's future lurked a few floors below
in the outpatient oncology waiting room,
a place close enough to hell to read the sign above its entrance.
A place where the blind sisters spin.

Soon enough he would become a waiter and watcher
in those regions and learn its lessons.

The lesson of Prometheus, for instance.
The reason human beings lack foresight is that,
if they had it, they would have no hope.
The lesson he learned only when it was too late.

Achieving cancer mastery is managing to love and be loved.
For this, one needs to learn to value waiting for its own sake.
One needs to endure overhearing others in the world of chairs
weeping on their cell phones, lingering helpless until denial
is finally broken and retreats in disarray.

Uphill Speech

A word about mercy.

She grapples with downhill speech and cries out,
cruelly spurred on as uphill speech beckons in her mind.
But just as what she wants to say
comes to the tip of her tongue,
she falls backward, exhausted by what uphill speech
extracts. She wills to hear the words flowing in her voice
and the ascension of them singing to me.

She wills. You look and listen. To no avail.
Why has she been condemned to this labor of Sisyphus?

Sentences, even whole paragraphs,
get compacted into single words
and someone you love offers with her tongue
meager meanings, while her face
entreats you to understand what's left inside.

You respond engagingly, of course. What
you say is quite right. Yes, I'll do it right away.

A word about despair.

At such times, you may sense
that you are far along the pathway of loss
and that you have sustained a deep bruise
that bleeds underneath but has not yet discolored the skin
with which you conceal your face.

Truth to tell, you brush the hidden bruise aside with busyness:
Did. Do. Done. Repeat.

A word about the unexpected.

You brush the hurts aside as one rubs an elbow
hit by a screen door closing faster than you thought it would
or a knee struck by a table,
a careless housekeeper, or a distracted friend,
moved slightly into the route your body charted long ago
through the darkened kitchen late at night.

Someone asks about her uphill speech and your grief
because you often smile and seem content.
You say that hurt has faded but not healed.

In truth and in a word, your hurt has seeped so deep
it no longer shows in the mirror in the morning
and for a moment without hurt looking back,
you nearly don't recognize yourself.

After You

We thought about Moses Herzog's madness
and behind that
the letter that Saul Bellow sent to his own death
and behind that
we thought about the novel as the enabler of death
and poetry as its nemesis.

As an afterthought, we wrote:
We have many deadlines to meet before we should die.
Signed it, sealed it, and put it in a drawer.

We were in agreement about this:
It is not the last day of living
that you should dread,
but the first day of dying.
The day you know that something unwelcome
can no longer be ignored.

In most of our time together,
I said, "After you."
It was just my bringing up talking.
Something said to please, with a wink.
Of all my suggestions you brushed aside,
why did you pick that one to follow?

Past Participle

Consisting of nothing beyond their shapes,
her wants were hard to know with certainty.
To him she said, or perhaps into her he read,
"I want." And then proceeded to list things
out of habit, for by that time
she knew that there was nothing
beneath the new dress, the ring,
the look, the touch, the spasm.

All that is its own shape and nothing more
is fleeting and fugitive.

For such a long time he gave her presents
when what she wanted was his presence.
Many men don't know the difference.
She would not have wanted them.

Presence was hard to locate.
Sometimes it was body, wholly body
with arms and hands that fill its sleeves.
At other times it was words that said
and sounds that signed on the dotted line.

His presence was clearly outlined with bold nib
but incomplete as such.
One of the worst pangs he could feel
would come as her presence faded
before his very eyes, one aspect at a time.

At My Door

Old man trouble rang the bell at my front door,
smiled when I opened it, said he was
selling encyclopedias. He came through.
I tried to demur and deny him at the time
but trouble won't be put off when he comes
and moves in.

Trouble stayed for a long time.
Weeks became months became years—
trouble travels in time and bends space
When he finally did leave
I didn't want him to go and was not sure
what I would do without him.

After that, I did not notice a change
except that I kept misplacing things.
That seemed odd because all my life
I have been a tidy person who believes that
you should put things back where they belong
when you finish with them,
so that you will never lose them.

I thought I left her sitting in a chair in a room
and returned to find someone else sitting there
or someone who wasn't there at all,
I wasn't sure which, just as I wasn't sure
if I had only misplaced or was finished with her.

I sift through the piles of knowledge
heaping in front of my bookcase,
the ink of their wisdom growing faint.
Every day there are fewer legible words on the pages
of the encyclopedia trouble gave me.

When they all finally go blank, will I?

To-Do List

There was a time, of long duration,
when my life was folded in half,
one time shared between two
in a place where two things
had to be done one at a time.

One thing was to care for her with myself
in her world of
two chairs she liked
in two rooms with
two television sets
one book of Sudoku puzzles
one bed
one commode.

That care was a prism
of touch and presence—
doing there and being there,
with reading poetry aloud
to her in between.

The other was to care for myself without her,
in my world of
chairs reserved for
reading and writing in

many rooms
many computers
many puzzles.

Those two cares were pacing in the not yet
on a station platform, awaiting the train
that has been announced
but hasn't arrived.

Those cares have released my voice
so I can refine speech
for poems as yet
unwritten and unread,
rather than watching the face
I had washed for her that morning
calling to me through the window
of a train pulling away.

A Country for Old Men

She came down with it
in her early sixties.
It.

She began to come down with it,
I should say. Began to be
brought down by it,
in her early sixties, not early eighties,
as might have been better form.
I daydreamed how it might have
made a difference if it had.
It.

Her incurable degenerative
chronic illness, brain tumor,
dark trespasser, stowaway,
hitchhiker one should not stop for.
We gave it many names.
It.

It brought decline, but also company.
Companionship previously unaccustomed.
Care with a price for which no fee was paid.
Mine.

There are two things you need to know.

One. We had been married
forty years when it moved in,
forty-eight when it outgrew
its quarters, and she died of it.
It.

Two. I stayed, and the merger
our marriage had become long before
was extended in a carceral process
that it directed, and we neither
courted nor controlled.
It.

I became her right hand,
then arm, then right leg,
then by and by,
pretty much everything
south of her waist.

After that, sometimes, in the off hours,
I'd wish we had stayed up north.
That would have given me more respite,
more unpaid caring hands in the neighborhood
in the New York we had made our own by then.

Perhaps the north would have given me that.
But I know it would have taken from her
the little time she had with our son and
with the baby, later the toddler
she got to know too little
during the little time she had.

So we merged and I became
her foundation and her movement,
and her needs became mine.
We dwelt and rearranged
ourselves in the commodious
prison-house we had bought,
soon enough cut in half by the stairway
she and I could not climb, not even together.
It.

Before I bought her out
and our merger was dissolved,
I'd begun to notice how other men
managed their own Its and how they
merged with someone loved
into unpaid caring.

They are rare sightings.
They stay mostly behind closed doors
and curtains drawn

against the glare of morning
or the melancholy of late afternoon.

Solitary walkers with shopping carts or pet dogs
or on occasional outings accompanied
by those who share their bodies
to restaurants, nail salons, hairdressers,
doctor's appointments.

They sport beards or stubble again,
abandoned since their twenties,
when they run out of reasons
to keep up appearances.

I admire old men who still
wear jackets and ties each day,
just in case they might drop by
the Yale Club for a quick drink
or a game of canasta or backgammon.

Such men are Covid scarce in these days,
as am I, of course, but it—that other It—
came as almost a relief by providing
shared burden, precaution, and hardship
as good reasons for shirking
the ordeals of making
chagrinned appearances

without giving up appearances,
when you or I, or both of us
were well along in giving them up,
and almost past caring.

The Irony of Loneliness

Once long ago,
just gazing at my
wife, more lovely
than I had ever imagined
a wife of mine would be,
I would undress her with
my mind. Taking her body out
and putting it where I wanted it to be.
She would notice that and remark
on the futility of my intent,
but I could imagine her smile.

Now she's gone, I see in the closet
the blouses, dresses, lingerie I once removed
and now I redress her with
my mind. Putting her body
back into where it once belonged.

Then I notice and remark, to myself, who else?,
on the irony of loneliness,
and I can imagine her smile.

Removing In

In the wake of passing speedboats and steadfast lovers,
you revel in waves that eventually retreat,
like the other guests, leaving hugs and promises received
with a gratitude that is requited
and expectations not false, merely exhausted.

In the ensuing quiet of the house, all rooms
are void but after a while will slowly refill
with sounds, smells, memories, scenes rectified
enabling busy talk, angry talk, pillow talk to resonate
once more in daydreams not punishing, only benign.

In all rooms but one, where no rearrangement
of bed and night table, no unpacking and repacking
of bureau drawers, no flower cutting and vaseing,
brings remontancy or palliates the bitter task of collecting her
clothing, body-bagged for donation not begrudging,
yet leaving more than closets empty.

Your posthumous home is a house,
one room smaller, into which you have re-moved
and where new living has reticulated,
where a varying voice talking to itself reverberates
down hallways and to one closed door where you return
each night, drawn by something constant.

Nightname

Being between
waiting and wanting—
let's say—to be found

Is someone calling your
name in the night?

A voice sound
pulling you from
a sound sleep?

pulled by her voice
distinct and clear—
let's say—to somewhere vague

calling Come, I need you
yet not saying where.

Being between
pointed and pointless—
let's say—to find

Is the calling voice
that awakens you—
let's say—revenant breath?

backtalk in the world
of the awake?

When dreaming
sometimes it sounds
with uncanny clarity

startled, you have learned
to tell it from reverberation
or murmur in your sleep.

Being summoned in this way
you are a page in a book torn out
on which an urgent intention has been written

Being between
removed and replaced—
let's say—from within

You hear only your nightname
followed by a silent conversation

Being between
I am here and here I am
find me and I'm coming
waiting and wanting—
let's say—to be alone.

Suddenly is Considerate

To disappear suddenly is considerate,
to do so piecemeal is cruel.

At first her presence was merely less definite.
Not being there in some ways
made her all the more there in others,
as the morning fog lifts
and confirms the tops of trees.
On the witness stand the evidence of her
would not be unimpeachable.

One morning he got into the car.
The day before he had tossed a paper
on the passenger's seat and left
sunglasses unfolded beside it.
Yet he found the glasses carefully closed
lying with the lenses up facing up—
she always worried about scratches—
and the paper neatly folded beside them.
This is something he might have done
without remembering, but so might she.

Nashville Snow

I don't know why the snow bothers to fall in Nashville.
It works hard all night to make a morning show.
The honkytonk musicians at least get to sleep sometimes,
but there is no closing time for Nashville snow.
If it manages to lay down five inches or six overnight,
few awaken to a sense of its beauty and peace,
and most are irate at the inconvenience.
They all have other places to go in order to be somewhere.

Somewhere up north she and I would arise before dawn
to shovel a path down the driveway so we could drive away
later, after the plows had come and cleared the street.

At that hour and in that company, we had the world alone
in a cold that could be touched as well as felt
and in a togetherness similarly sensuous.
This was a gift silent and secret enough
to overcome loneliness. The snow partook of that with us,
and each descending flake seemed less alone.

After shoveling, people say words like drifting, heavy, light,
dry powder for skiing or wet packing for snowmen
We reflected on something else over cups of cocoa.
The essence of snow, we agreed, is the silence of its falling
and its secrets whispered to us

as we threw it into the clearing of the world.

Thus we used to work gloved and muffled
in the darkness of cold air
and watched the light in the east come up
over the trees and the roof of the house that was our home.

Living Will

My daughter and I mulled it over.
My remaining life would pass with decency and dignity,
weather permitting.
In a style modest and optimistic.
I smiled.

No, she said, optimism is a proposition.
The word hovered between us,
we watched it leave.
Hope then, I said, which is a posture.

In a style humble and hopeful,
a Shaker style for the furniture of mind
and heart aging in smaller quarters.
I smiled again.

Your mind is too ornate, she said,
would the simplicity suit you?

I hope to outlive that opposition, I replied.
What I look for ahead is not
simple, but only more compressed.
I want my space and my time to line up.

I see. Icons without iconology, exuberance
under the breath. This time she smiled.

Now you're catching on. Attention
that deserves payment without
calling attention to itself.

She seemed distracted, then said
A cleaner line,
cleaner than a rhyme.

Just so, I said.

The sound the smooth curve of a railing
makes as the hand slides
along it, but you can't quite hear.

The shaping of space
between parallel slats in a door
or as a design element
decorative, but not dominant.

A natural wood stain,
reveals the gift of grain,
its lines showing something
pure, but not pristine.

She searched for a question.
Hygiene? Another posture?
She smiled again.

No, I'd say such shapes were sturdy
geometries of consolation
to their makers,
offered to celebrate
a creation, but not their own.

And one that is not ours. Shapes sufficient, she said,
unto the day, I answered.

Handles and knobs
that do not menace or repel
invite the embrace of human flesh;

chairs not so comfortable
as to let you sit too long
or neglect your chores;

just enough glass in doors
to reveal something
within, but not too much.

Claim the Space

To be solid is to claim space and take it up.

I forgot what solid feels like,
but it would come back to me,
would firm and shape me
intact from the inside out

not the outside in.
At such times I forgot that
I was merely remembering
my life, not living it.

I walk an unfamiliar trail and stalk
someone who is merely ambling
yet increasing the distance between us.
I thought by being solid I could attain her.

If I catch up to her, where will I be; and what?
If I lose sight of her, I'm afraid I will dissipate
and float awhile before being weighed down
in the space of the solid world again,
but by then she will be gone.

Holding on to Morning

"Grandma is on a trip."

My grandson said this in his quiet eight year old voice,
and I said, "What makes you say that?"

"Because I have not talked to her in a long time.
We used to talk and she would listen
to as much as I could tell.
I always had to stop before she was ready.
I couldn't sit still long in those days, you remember?"

I did.
"She had more listening in her than anyone else," I said.

"Yes," he warmed to that, "and now I want
to tell her more things to make up for how little
I told her then. Either she is on a trip and cannot hear me
or she is here and does not want to listen to me anymore.
That would make me sad, so I think she is on a trip.
But then, I get lonesome and wish I knew when
she was coming back."

"Buddy, you know Grandma died."

"I know. I talked with her about that at the time. She told me how not to be sad, but she said she could not teach me how not to be lonesome. But I wish I knew when she was coming back. She told me that being dead does not keep someone you love from coming back home."

The Way of All Bruising

I walk barefoot in my house
to respect wooden floors,
hard but still vulnerable.
I savor feeling them on my soles,
the unsullied smoothness.

I walk barefoot in my house
to respect the place of dwelling,
as my son, who has lived in Japan
and knows, advised me to do.

When the gravity and weight
of existence slipped one day
from my left hand and landed
on an exposed toenail,
it hurt a short while, and left
a dark stain that has lingered
or perhaps loitered.

A bruise, a pool of dried blood,
I can only suppose. As a child
I accidentally struck something hard
against a fingernail and then
watched for weeks as the mark
rose upward as the nail grew.

Finally the bruise was trimmed away.

Our cells all come and go, completely
turning over every few years,
I forget how many, but compared
with other endings and new beginnings,
it is quick. Still, this process now seems
to take longer. Blood stains tend to linger
longer as attachment turns into acquaintance.

When the bruise beneath the nail neared
the cutoff point the blood itself
seemed reluctant to leave me to the rest of my life,
as is the way of all bruising.

I have reached a time of vigilance concerning
black and grainèd spots rising imperceptibly
from below to reveal themselves on my skin.
Some bumps and nodules ride away eventually
on transport caused by the colliding and jostling of cells
so that my metabolism is a magic lantern show
and my body a waystation of passing along.

No matter how closely watched, toward the end
the body becomes a place of debarkation
for things deciding to settle and colonize,
to overgrow and press against and strangle,

flesh present contending against flesh past,
as is the way of all bruising.

Random Walk

Living human life is to live
> in a world of labyrinths with one way in
> and one out
>> whose turnings and cul de sacs change
> position randomly as you wander toward perhaps
> the exit.

Random walks are our saving grace,
> a path of passing joy today, disappointment
> tomorrow.
>> Maps and memories are of no avail in labyrinths
> and in lives that don't hold still.

Lives led
> where you pursue yourself
>> while seeming to be pursuing others
> who may not want to be found.

Lives led
> in mazes of thick hedgerow traversed by
>> following blind turnings leading
> to places wrongly imagined.

From Leyden jars, arcing energy twists
              prods and jolts us
while we walk barefoot on damp ground.

Some run their course sooner than others.
Thoroughfares open as they approach
groping in the dark
for reasons, we cannot understand.

Morning is given to mourners still en route,
who walk down ways they find blocked,
try a new path until again they must halt.

In our mazes, we lose our way and choose it at the same time.
The paths followed, follow us
with an uncanny sense—between a thought and a recollection—
that we might have gone that way before.

Still, as you pass, you try and fail to recall
if those now cutting you are the same
sharp pointed leaves you have brushed against before
or the same thorns you embraced and that embraced you
the last time you faltered and grew weary.

Remontancy

Marriage and parentage behind,
Freedom as you please ahead.
Where do you turn?

Master of meaning
No need to persuade.
Who's there as you walk alone?

Escaping friction is your fiction.
It has no traction, so you flail
without moving forward.
Does the stasis of your life become you?

Early morning sun blue bright
after the ice storm.
Step into a diamond,
marvel a crystalline world.
For no reason you go to a mailbox
you rent for no reason.
Will you open the letter you hope to find?

Widower's Watch

A widow gets the topmost room
of houses above the harbors
of New Bedford and Martha's Vineyard,
where she recalls watching over the waves and awaiting
the man whose life she has shared with the sea.

A widower watches in the basement room
and remembers how the woman anchored their household.
In this room, a wash tub stands dry and idle,
and Ball Jars of preserves she put up sit patiently on shelves.
She worked from below. He feels the buried supports
of the life she provided for him. They still give him footing,
and they remind him of the subterranean strength of her love.

Widows watch for one who will not arrive.
Widowers adrift at sea long to be watched for again.

Acknowledgments

I am a teacher who writes about philosophy by day and loves poetry by night. I have relentlessly pressed poems upon so many that I cannot name them all. But I am especially grateful to Millie Solomon, Lauren Kuratko, and many friends and colleagues over the years at the Center for Humans and Nature. In addition, in the arts and medicine poetry group at Vanderbilt Medical School, my many discerning readers have included Brian Christman, Daniel Birchmore, and Brenda Butka. At the Poets from the Neighborhood group in Williamson County, Tennessee, David M. Harris and Veera Rajaratnam have improved my work irresistibly. The closest I have to siblings are my cousins—William Conrad and his wife Judy; and Joseph Conrad and his wife Nancy—and they have left their marks on the poems in this book in ways both large and small. And finally, I remember and acknowledge two dear poet friends, who passed away shortly after my wife did, Kathleen Cochran and Joan Gibb Engel.

About The Author

Bruce Jennings teaches and writes on ethical and social issues in healthcare at Vanderbilt University. He is the author of several books on topics such as end-of-life care, hospice and palliative care, long-term care and chronic disability, and health equity and justice. His poetry, like his work on ethics, responds to belonging, caring, aging, love, and loss. This is his first published volume of poetry.